STEP BY STEP HOW TO CREATE MULTI OPERATING SYSTEMS (OS) IN ONE COMPUTER OR VIRTUAL MACHINE (VIRTUALBOX) USING MASTERBOOTER

OS Case Study: MS-DOS, Linux Mint
And Microsoft Windows

ARYANTO

This book formatting template was made by Derek Murphy of Creativindie Design;

STEP BY STEP HOW TO CREATE MULTI OPERATING SYSTEMS (OS) IN ONE
COMPUTER OR VIRTUAL MACHINE (VIRTUALBOX) USING MASTERBOOTER
Copyright © 2016 by Aryanto.

For information contact :
http://aryanto165.com

Book and Cover design by Aryanto (Adazing.com)
ISBN paper from createspace.com
ISBN-13 : 978-1536881820
ISBN-10: 1536881821

ISBN ebook from draft2digital.com
ISBN(s) for ebook: 9781536535716

First Edition: August 2016

CONTENTS

Chapter One

How to Make a USB Flashdisk
bootable Under DOS

FIRSTLY, MAKE SURE YOU HAVE a USB Flashdisk with minimal size 4 GB. Here's step by step how to make a USB Flashdisk bootable under DOS.

1. We need to download some software applications required below. You can extract them to the location or folder that you want.

   - **Hpflash1**. Used to format a USB Flashdisk, so we can insert **Windows 98 MS-DOS file systems**. Download links:
     - http://www.sevenforums.com/attachments/tutorials/42022d1260810265-ms-dos-bootable-flash-drive-create-hpflash1.zip

- or you can use this link (mirror): http://downloads.ziddu.com/download/25447740/hpflash1.zip.html

- **Win98boot.zip**. This file contains Windows 98 MS-DOS file systems. Download links:
  - http://www.sevenforums.com/attachments/tutorials/42023d1260810265-ms-dos-bootable-flash-drive-create-win98boot.zip
  - or you can use this link (mirror): http://downloads.ziddu.com/download/25447744/pm80.zip.html

- **Pm80.zip (PowerQuest Partition Magic)**. Used to create and modification your harddisk partition. Download link: http://downloads.ziddu.com/download/25447744/pm80.zip.html

- **Part240.zip (Ranish Partition Manager)**. Same as **pm80** application, this application is also useful to create a partition on your harddisk. However, this application is not good enough to be used to make the first partition at the beginning. we use this application to activate or hide the desired partition, in addition, we also use this application to mark the partition which is used as the boot (for start up your computer system). Download links:
  - http://www.ranish.com/part/
  - or you can use this link (mirror):

http://downloads.ziddu.com/download/254477
43/part240.zip.html (*Recommended*)

- **Nc.zip (Norton Commander)**. This application we use to make copy / remove / delete folder or file like Windows Explorer application. But only running on a MS-DOS system. Download links:
  - https://winworldpc.com/product/norton-commander/5x
  - or you can use this link (mirror): http://downloads.ziddu.com/download/2544774 2/nc.zip.html (*recommended*)
- **Mrboot.zip (MasterBooter)**. Master Booter is a small application to handle many OS in One Computer. With this application we can easily select which operating system to be turned on (running) or off. Not only that, we can also hide certain operating systems, providing a password and others that can not be easily accessed by an intruder (or other users). Download links:
  - http://masterbooter.com/download/sharewarev ersion_en.html
  - or you can use this link (mirror) http://downloads.ziddu.com/download/2544774 1/mrboot.zip.html

all risk of use of the above applications is the responsibility of your own. ***I am just giving an explanation*** *of the use of these applications to help facilitate you to install a variety OS (Operating Systems) desired in your personal computer.*

2.   After all applications downloaded and extracted. *For example, I put all the applications in the folder* **d:\resources**. Follow the instructions below to install the application **hpflash**.

- If you used Windows XP, double click to file **hpflash1.exe** or if you are running on Windows 7/8/10, you can right click on the mouse button and choose **Run as administrator** menu.

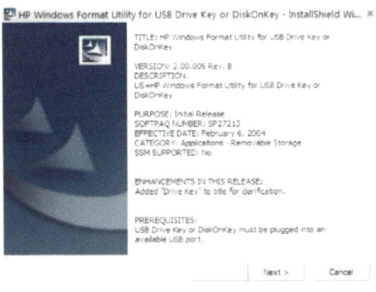

Figure 1.1. Install Hpflash - 01

- Click the next button (**Next >**).

- In the license agreement window tick the sentence "*I accept the terms in the lincense agreement*" selection radio button and then click the next button (**Next >**).

Figure 1.2. Install Hpflash - 02

- In the **InstallShield Wizard** window click the next button again

Figure 1.3. Install Hpflash - 03

- In **the license agreement**, click the Yes Button.

Figure 1.4. Install Hpflash - 04

- In **the Choose Destinatoin Location**, click the Next Button.

Figure 1.5. Install Hpflash - 05

- Then wait a while until the program window **display the InstallShield Wizard complete**. Click the Finish button.

Figure 1.6. Install Hpflash - 06

- Following completion of the install process, you can find the icon on the desktop as shown below.

Figure 1.7. Install Hpflash - 07

3. Connect your USB Flashdisk into your computer.

4. Run the **HP USB Disk Storage Format Tool** application that was just installed (or you can double click the icon as shown on figure 1.7).

If you are using **Windows 7/8/10** *as the operating system, right click button mouse on the icon and choose* **Run as administrator***.*

5. Choose your USB Flashdisk device from the drop down list at the top.

6. Choose **FAT32** as the file system.

Figure 1.8. Making bootable USB Flashdisk-01

7. Then tick **Quick Format** and **Create a DOS startup disk** are located under **Format options**.

8. Click triple dot ("...") button at *using DOS system files*

located at to determine the location of Windows 98 system files.

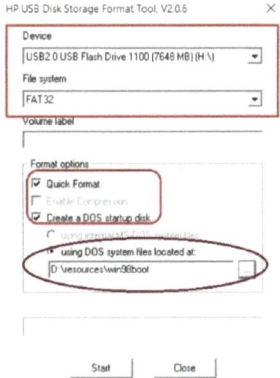

Figure 1.9. Making bootable USB Flashdisk-02

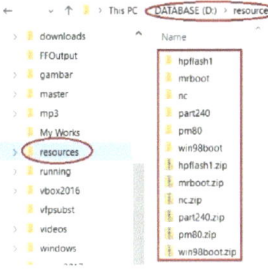

Figure 1.10. Example location download and extract

As shown at **figure 1.10**, I extract **win98boot.zip** to path / folder d:\resources. So in **figure 1.9**, we get path / folder as seen below:

d:\resource\win98boot.

9.   Then click the **start** button to begin the process of formatting and installation of the windows 98 system boot.

10. If you get warning message, click **Yes** button to continue

the process.

Figure 1.11. Making bootable USB Flashdisk-03

11.   Wait until the displayed message that the formatting process and the installation completed.

Figure 1.12. Making bootable USB Flashdisk-04

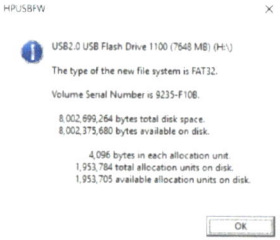

Figure 1.13. Making bootable USB Flashdisk-05

12.   Now, you can copy other applications (folders: **mrboot**, **nc**, **part240**, **pm80** and **win98boot**) into your bootable USB Flashdisk.

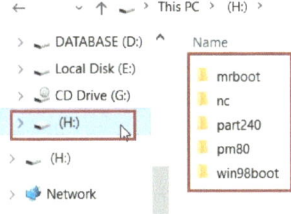

Figure 1.14. Making bootable USB Flashdisk-06

There are three pieces of the file system that does not look. They are **command.com**, **io.sys** and **msdos.sys**. Usually 3 pieces of files that are protected by the Windows system. But, if you want to see these files, you must unhide them from menu View Option (Windows Explorer). See figure below:

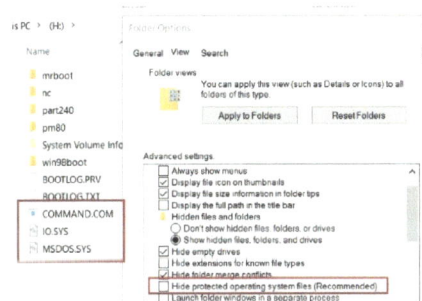

Figure 1.14b. Unhide Protected System files

13. Now, try to boot your computer using this bootable USB Flashdisk. Do not forget to arrage BIOS of your computer in order to boot via USB Flashdisk.

```
Microsoft(R) Windows 98
   (C)Copyright Microsoft Corp 1981-1998.

C:\>_
```

Figure 1.15. Windows 98 MS-DOS Systems-01

```
Microsoft(R) Windows 98
   (C)Copyright Microsoft Corp 1981-1998.

C:\>dir/w

 Volume in drive C has no label
 Volume Serial Number is 9235-F10B
 Directory of C:\

[PMB0]       [MRBOOT]        [NC]             [PART240]
        0 file(s)             0 bytes
        4 dir(s)      7,626.03 MB free

C:\>_
```

Figure 1.16. Windows 98 MS-DOS Systems-02

Chapter Two

Make Partitions and Install MS-DOS in Real
Computer or using Virtual Machine
(Virtualbox)

AFter we create bootable USB Flashdisk, Now *the next step are To Make Partition and Install MS-DOS as the first Operationg System in your harddisk.* Prepare a personal computer or laptop that will be used as the experimental material. In addition to a laptop or personal computer, you can also use a virtual machine to try this step. I use a laptop Asus GL552V type and installed *Oracle VM*

VirtualBox (virtual machine) that can be downloaded in https://www.virtualbox.org.

*If you are **new to working on creating the partition** on the harddisk, I suggest to use a virtual machine before trying on a real computer.*

Now, here's step by step to make partitions and install MS-DOS as the Operating Systems.

1. **In real computer**, prepare a personal computer or laptop.

2. **In Virtual Machine** (if you use a real computer skip this step). So, you can follow the steps below to install the virtual machine.

    a. Download VirtualBox Application from https://www.virtualbox.org.

Figure 2.1. Download Virtualbox

    b. Download ***VirtualBox 5.1.2 for Windows*** and ***Extension Pack***.

    c. And then, install VirtualBox into your computer. You just follow the step to install it.

d. Running VirtualBox with **Run as Administrator** mode.

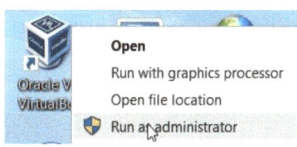

Figure 2.2. Running VirtualBox with Run as Administrator Mode

e. After Finished, add *Extension Pack* into your VirtualBox. You can add *extension pack* with double click to that file.

f. You can change the **default storage location** virtualbox via the menu preferences (click menu *File->References*).

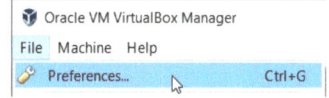

Figure 2.3a. Create New Virtual Machine - 01

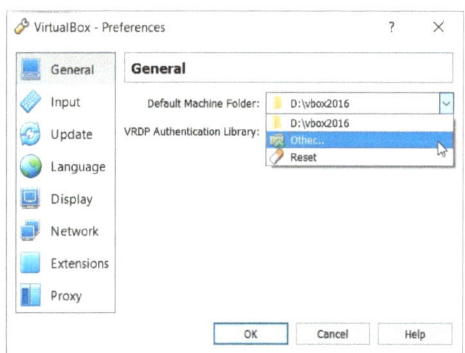

Figure 2.3b. Create New Virtual Machine - 01

g. If You already choose, where to save your virtual

machine, and then click *Machine* menu, and choose *New* to create New Virtual Machine.

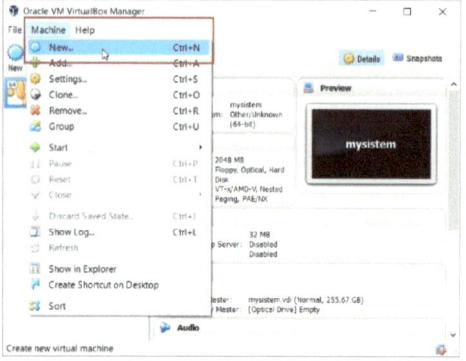

Figure 2.3c. Create New Virtual Machine – 01

h. In ***the Name and Operating System*** windows, specify the name, type and version of the virtual machine as desired. Or you can follow the fields as shown below.

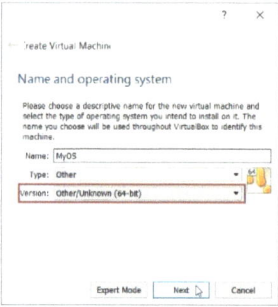

Figure 2.4. Name and Operating System

Name: **MyOS**

Type: **Other**

Version: **Other/Unknown (64-bit)**

i. Click the Next Button.

j. In ***the memory Size*** windows, select the amount of

memory (RAM) in megabytes to be allocated to the virtual machine. The Recommended memory size is **64 MB**. But, if your computer have bigsize of memory, I suggest 1024 MB or 2048 MB RAM.

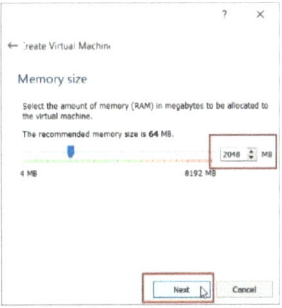

Figure 2.5. Memory Size

k. Click the Next Button.

l. In *the Hard Disk* windows, click The Create Button.

Figure 2.6. Hard Disk Windows

m. In *the Hard disk file type* windows, click The Next Button.

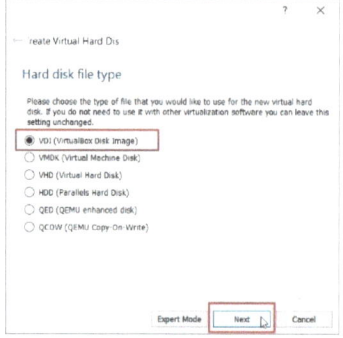

Figure 2.7. Hard Disk File Type

n. In ***the Storage on physical hard disk*** windows, click the Next Button again.

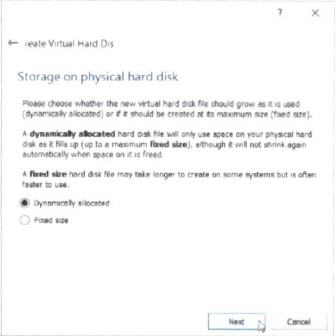

Figure 2.8. Storage on physical hard disk Window

o. Finally, in ***the File location and size*** window, select the size of the virtual hard disk to ± 100 GB (*recommended*). And then, click the Create button.

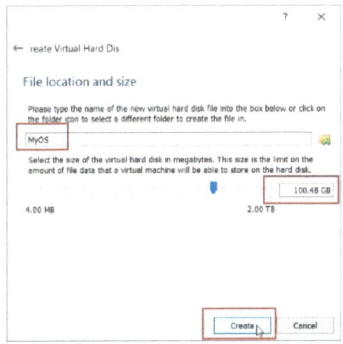

Figure 2.9. File location and size Window

p.   Now, we just have a virtual machine with 100 GB size of harddisk.

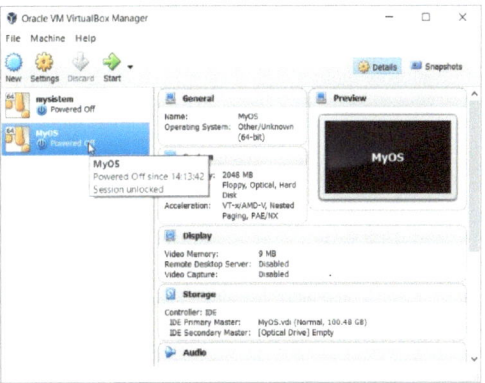

Figure 2.10. List of Virtual Machine

In Figure 2.10, I have two virtual machine. The new virtual machine name is **MyOS**.

3.   Restart your computer with bootable USB Flashdisk.

3.1. For **the real computer**, you just set the settings on your computer's BIOS to boot via USB Flashdisk. If nothing wrong, you can see on screen like figure 1.15.

3.2. For **the Virtual Machine**, we need some setting so that the virtual machine can boot by using a USB Flashdisk.

a. Connect your bootable USB Flashdisk into your computer.

b. Open the Computer Management. In this windows, check the label of bootable usb flashdisk.

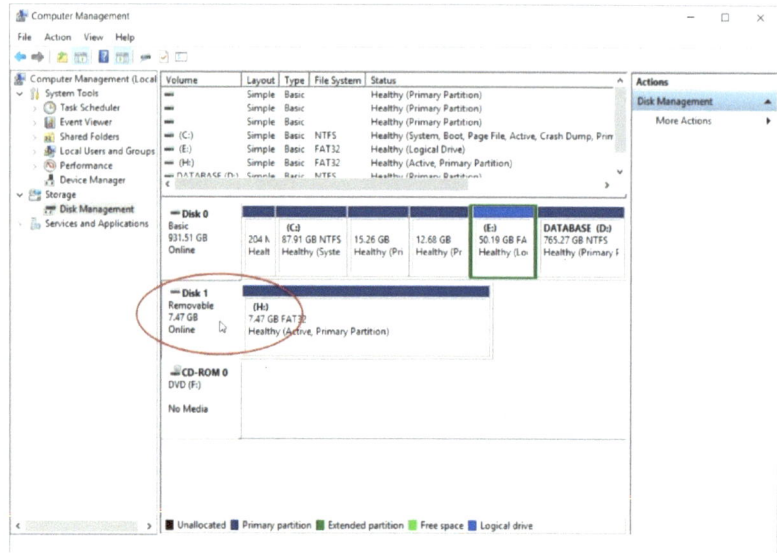

Figure 2.11. Label of bootable usb flashdisk

c. Create a virtual disk for access usb flashdrive. Follow the steps below.

- Open Command Prompt application from your desktop using ***Run as administrator***.

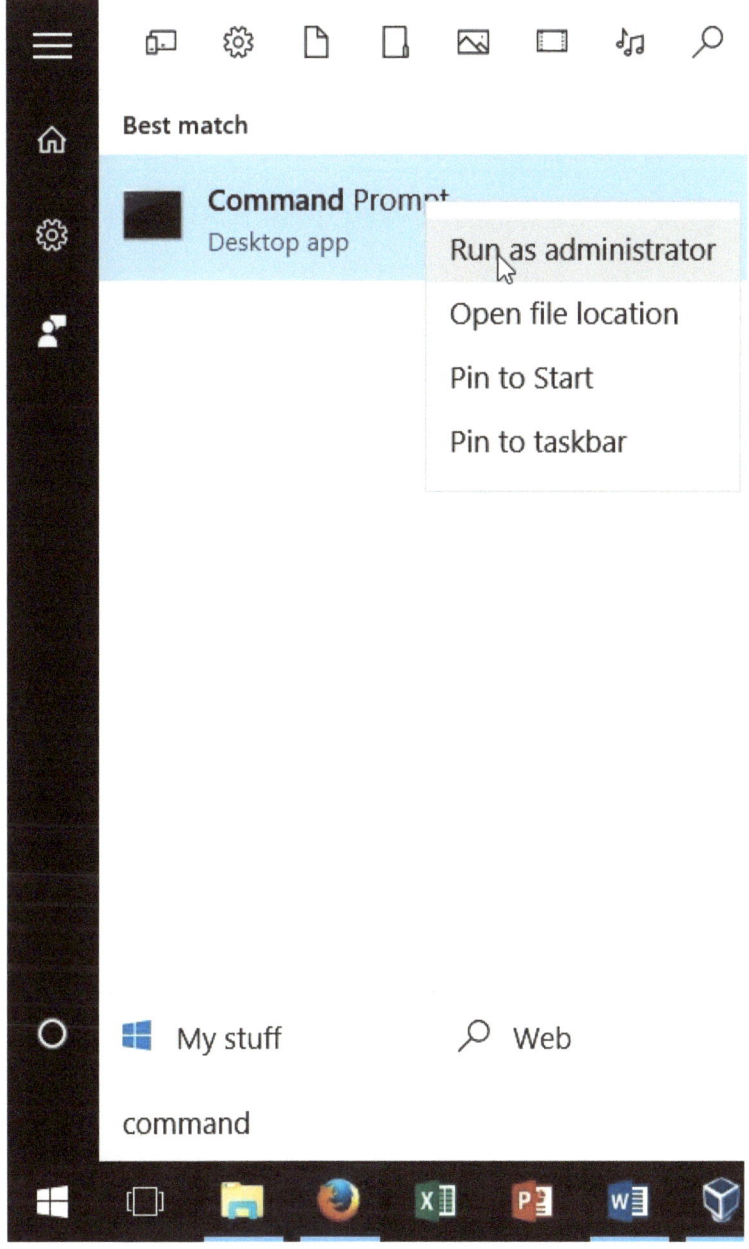

Figure 2.12. Open Command Prompt Application

- Type the coding below to change path or folder.

```
Cd\program files\oracle\virtualbox
```

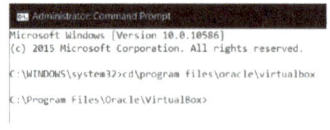

Figure 2.13. Change Drive (CD) to Virtualbox location install

The path your type above is depends on the virtualbox install location, because we want to use internal command from **vboxmanage** application file.

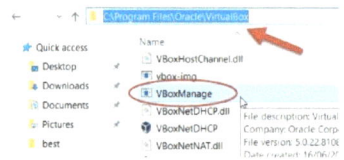

Figure 2.14. Virtualbox location install

- If figure 2.13 is shown, type the coding below to start creating virtual usb flashdisk. Do not press Enter key, until you type the last word 'physicaldrive1'

```
vboxmanage    internalcommands    createrawvmdk    -filename
d:\usb_disk1.vmdk -rawdisk \\.\physicaldrive1
```

You can change d:\usb_disk1.vmdk location to where do you want it.

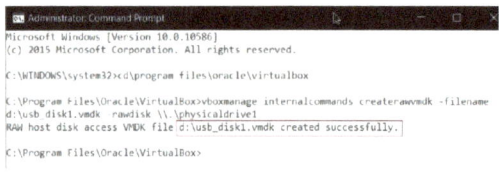

Figure 2.15. Creating virtual disk for access usb flashdisk

- You can see in drive **d:** file **usb_disk1.vmdk** now.

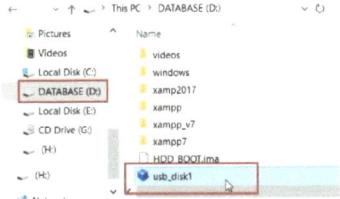

Figure 2.16. Usb virtual disk file

- Please backup / copy this file (usb_disk1.vmdk) to the other location.
- Close Command Prompt Windows.

d. Back to the Oracle VM Virtualbox Manager windows, click the setting button to set our *MyOS* Machine or you can use right click on it.

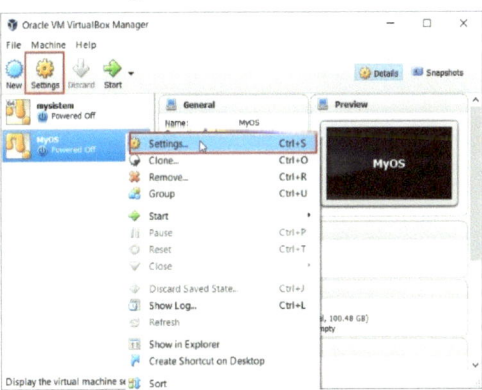

Figure 2.17. Setting of Virtual Machine

e. Click *Storage* menu in left corner.

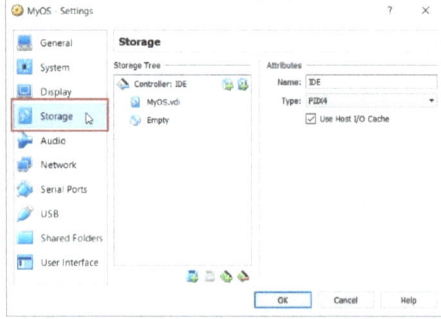

Figure 2.18. Setting of Virtual Machine

f.   Make sure the bootable usb flashdisk connected to a computer again. To add a virtual hard drive in the form of the bootable usb flashdisk click **the adds new storage attachmen** button.

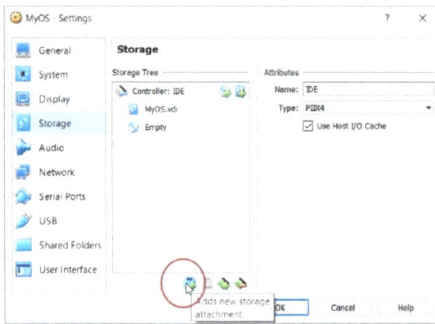

Figure 2.19. Adds new storage attachment

g.   Click **Add Hard Disk**.

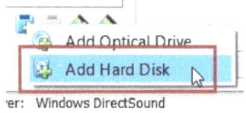

Figure 2.20. Add Hard Disk

h. In **the virtualbox – question** window, click the **choose existing disk** button.

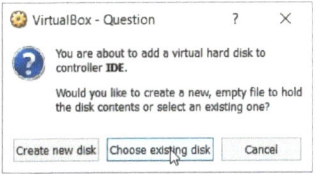

Figure 2.21. VirtualBox - Question

i. Choose **usb_disk1** file and click the open button.

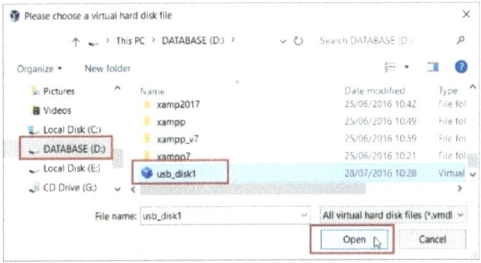

Figure 2.22. Choose a virtual hard disk file

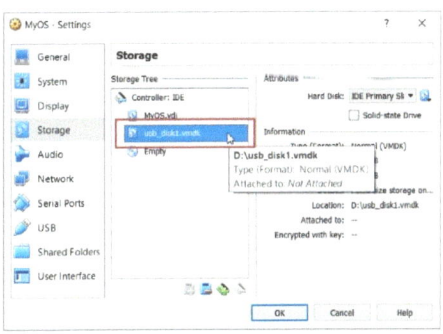

Figure 2.23. Storage tree window

j. Click **MyOS.vdi** from the controller and Change MyOS.vdi attributes to **IDE Secondary Slave**.

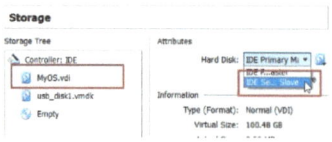

Figure 2.24. Change Hard Disk Attributes

k. Click **usb_disk1.vmdk** and change attributes to **IDE Primary Master**.

Figure 2.24. Change usb_disk1 Attributes

l. Click MyOS.vdi again and change attributes to **IDE Primary Slave**. So now, we have a **usb_disk1.vmdk** as IDE Primary Master and **MyOS.vdi** as IDE Primary Slave.

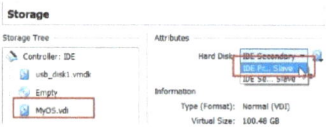

Figure 2.26. Change MyOS Attributes

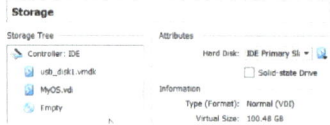

Figure 2.27. Final list of Storage

m. Click the **OK** button to save the setting.

n. Click the Start button from the top menu to start MyOS

Virtual Machine.

Figure 2.28. The Start Button

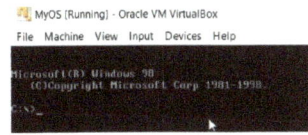

Figure 2.29. MyOS running on MSDOS

If you click on the Virtualbox Windows area, your mouse will be in that window. **To get your mouse back to Windows** (to exit mouse from virtualbox windows), *press* **right CTRL** *in your* **keyboard**.

o.   The figure 2.29 have the same look as the personal computer boot.

In the next step, **because the settings (installation steps) on virtualbox is the same as the settings on the personal computer,** *then the explanation will be done only on virtualbox, but you can do it on a personal computer..*

Before we continue, I would like to explain to you the plan of partition we will make. Now, we have a 100 GB virtual machine disk, we will divide it as the table below.

Table 2.1.
The Divide of Virtual Machine Disk

Size	Partition Type	Utilities
Primary Partition		
± 200 MB	Primary Partition	Using as DOS or MS-DOS Operating Systems
± 20 GB	Primary Partition	Using as Windows XP Operating Systems
Extended Partiton		
± 20 GB	Logical Partition	Using as Linux Mint Operating Systems
± 59 GB	Logical Partition	Using as Data / Database

In accordance with table 2.1, then the partition divided into 3 parts, 2 primary partition and one extended partition. we can make a maximum of four primary partitions, but because we are using **the trial version of masterbooter** application then we can only use a maximum of three partitions only.

4. Because we use **the empty virtual hard disk**, so we can start to create some partition now. Type this code below to open *Partiton Magic Application.*

```
Cd\pm80
Pqmagic
```

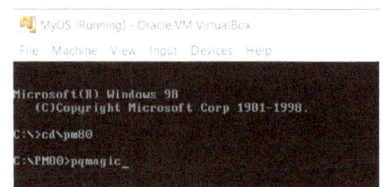

Figure 2.30. Make Partition - 01

*If we have not empty hard disk, for example in a real computer or personal computer, we must delete all of the partition using **part240** application. So do not forget to backup your data. At the end of this chapter, i explain to you how to delete partition using part240 application.*

5.   If you got error like below, press 'i' key from keyboard to ignore.

```
Critical Error: Abort, Retry, Ignore, Fail?
```

6.   In **the PowerQuest PartitionMagic 8.0** window, change your disk1 (usb) to disk2 (virtual hard disk).

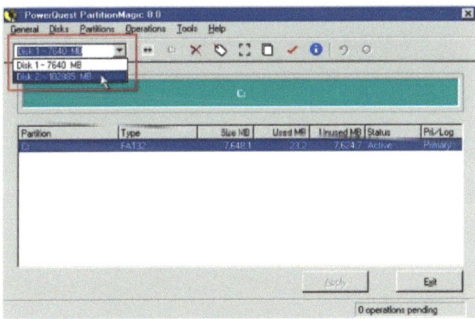

Figure 2.31. Make Partition - 02

7.   And then, click *Operations, Create* menus, or you can right-click on the top of partition.

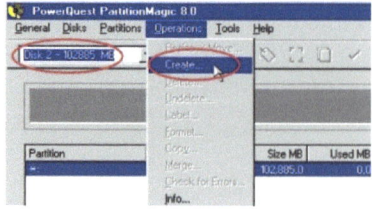

Figure 2.32. Make Partition – 03 (Operatons, Create menus)

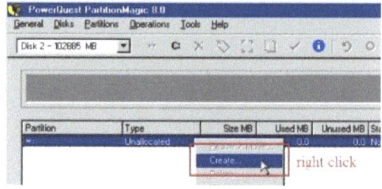

Figure 2.33. Make Partition – 04 (Right-click)

8.   Choose and click **Create** menu. And then program will show to you a create partition windows.

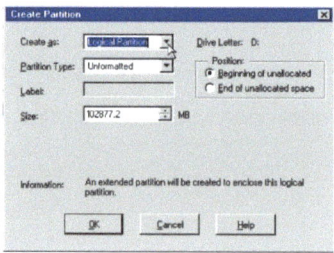

Figure 2.34. Make Partition – 05

9.   In create partition window, you set the form input like figure below.

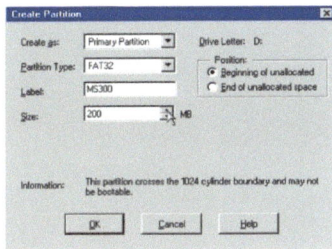

Figure 2.35. Make Partition – 06

Create as: **Primary Partition**

Partition Type: **FAT32**

Label: **MSDOS**

Size: **200**

To get **the right SIZE** press the up and down arrows, so in my virtualbox now i get **203.9** MB size.

Figure 2.36. Make Partition – 07

10.   Click **the OK button** to save the changes.

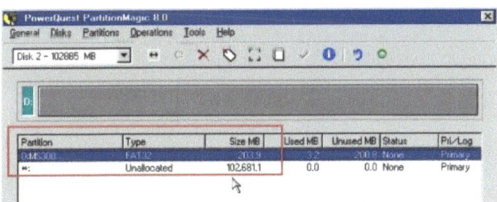

Figure 2.37. Make Partition – 08

11.   Next, Right-Click to **Unallocated** type to make a second partition.

12.   Choose and click **Create** menu.

13.   For a second partition, you can set the form input like figure below.

Figure 2.38. Make Partition – 09

Create as: **Primary Partition**

Partition Type: **FAT32**

Label: **WINXP**

Size: **20000**

To get **the right SIZE** press the up and down arrows, so in my virtualbox now i get **20002.8** MB size (± 20 GB).

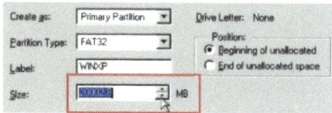

Figure 2.39. Make Partition – 10

14. Click the OK button to save the changes. Now, we already have 2 primary partition like the figure below.

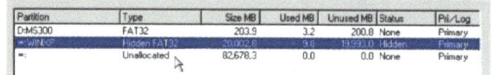

Figure 2.40. Make Partition – 11

15. The next, we will create the Extended partition. Right-click on the **unallocated** type partition.

16. Choose and click **create** menu again.

17. For the Firsts Extended partition, you can set like figure below.

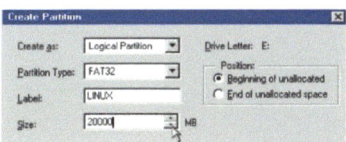

Figure 2.41. Make Partition – 12

Create as: **Logical Partition**

Partition Type: **FAT32**

Label: **LINUX**

Size: **20000**

To get **the right SIZE** press the up and down arrows, so in my virtualbox now i get **20002.8** MB size (± 20 GB).

18. Click the OK Button to save the changes.

19. Repeat steps 15-18 to make the last extended partition. Set form input like the figure below.

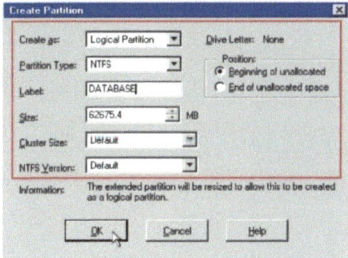

Figure 2.42. Make Partition – 13

Create as: **Logical Partition**

Partition Type: **NTFS**

Label: **DATABASE**

Because this is the last extended partition, so do not set the size of this partition. We use all the remaining size.

20. Click the OK button to save the changes. Now, all of the partition shown like below.

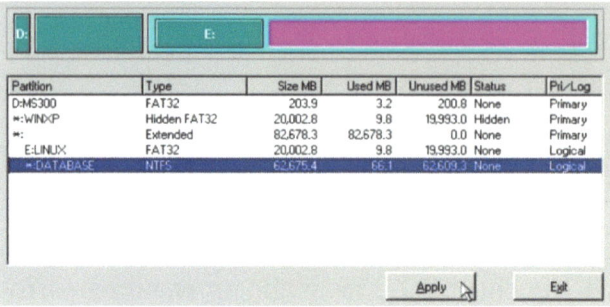

Figure 2.43. Make Partition – 14

21. Click the **Apply** button to start the process.

22. In **the Apply Changes** window, click the **Yes** button.

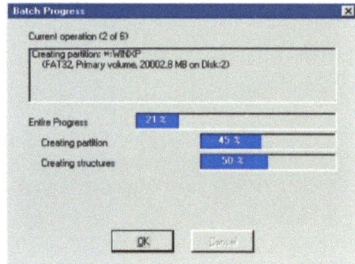

Figure 2.44. Make Partition – 15

23. Wait until all operations completed. And then click the Ok Button.

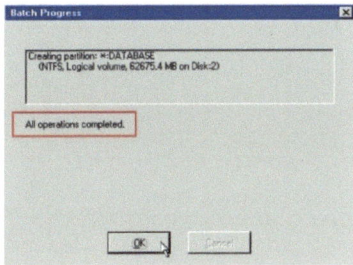

Figure 2.45. Make Partition – 16

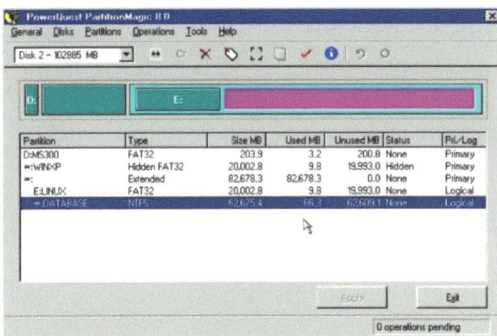

Figure 2.46. Make Partition – 17

24. The last steps is to make active MSDOS Partition. Right-click MSDOS Partition, choose **Advanced** menu, then click **set Active...** menu.

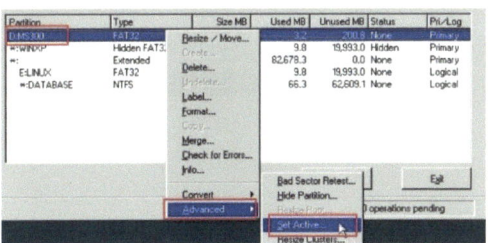

Figure 2.47. Make Partition – 18

25. In the **Set Active Partition** windows, click the OK button.

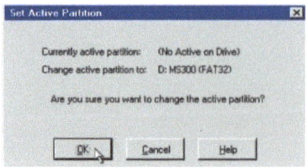

Figure 2.48. Make Partition – 19

26. Click the **Apply** button to start the process.

27. In **the Apply Changes** window, click the **Yes** button.

28. After that, in the **rebooting** windows, click **OK** button. Wait until you can see the 'C:\>' prompt like figure 2.29.

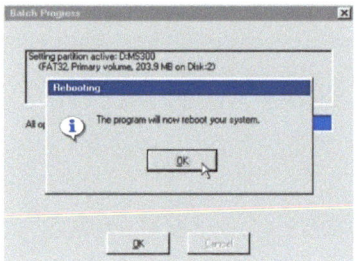

Figure 2.49. Make Partition – 20

29. You can type the coding below to format and insert MSDOS systems into MSDOS Partition (now active as drive D).

```
Cd\win98b~1
format d: /u /q /s
```

```
Microsoft(R) Windows 98
   (C)Copyright Microsoft Corp 1981-1998.

C:\>cd\win98b~1

C:\WIN98B~1>format d: /u /q /s_
```

Figure 2.50. Make Partition – 21

30. Press 'enter' key to start the format.

31. Press 'Y' key if the system need confirmation.

32. Wait until *format completed* and *system transferred*. And then, type MSDOS name to use as the volume label, then press 'enter' key to save it.

Figure 2.51. Make Partition – 22

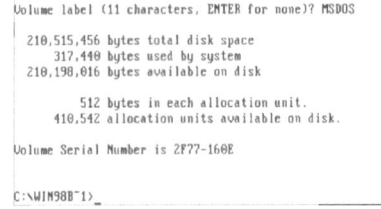

Figure 2.52. Make Partition – 23

33. Now we need to copy all of the folders and files system into drive D. So, type the coding below to open NC (*Norton Commander*) application to do that.

```
cd\nc
nc
```

In the NC window, we have two window, drive D (virtual disk) in the left window and C (usb) in right windows.

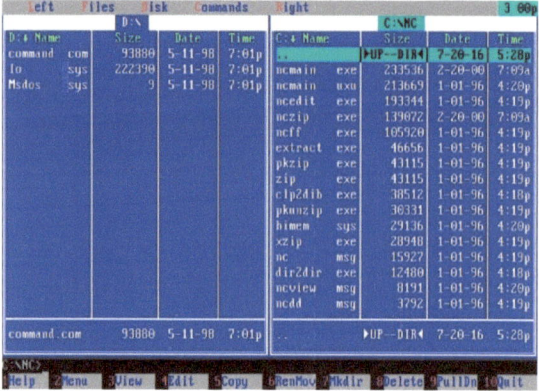

Figure 2.53. Make Partition – 24

34. Highlight '..' object in the right window, and press 'enter' key.

35. Now, klik the 'insert' key to mark folder **mrboot, nc, part240, pm80** and **win98b~1**.

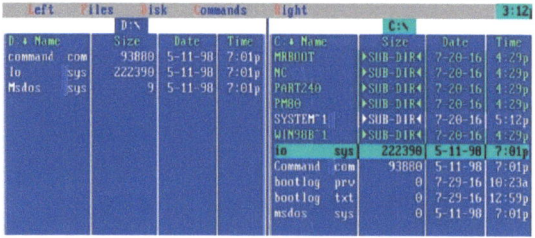

Figure 2.54. Make Partition – 25

36. And then press 'F5' in your keyboard to show copy window.

37. Press 'ALT+I' to mark '*include subdirectories*'.

Figure 2.55. Make Partition – 26

38. Press 'ALT+C' to start copy process. Wait until all of folder and files shown in left window (in drive D).

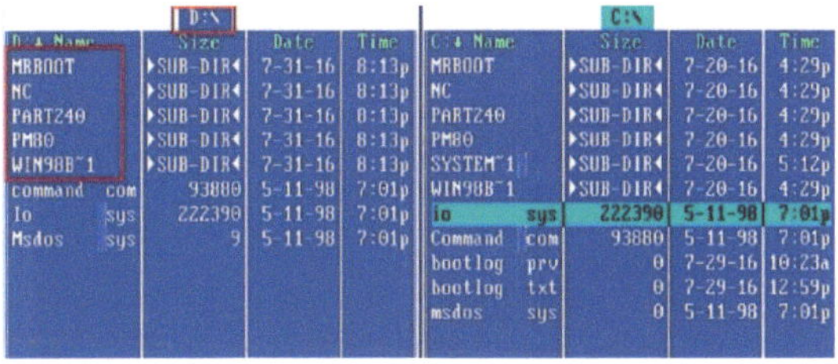

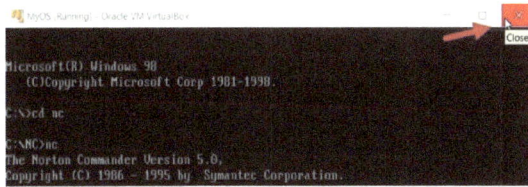

Figure 2.56. Make Partition – 27

39. Press 'F10' to Quit from NC Application.

40. Press 'Y' or choose Yes from the norton commander confirmation: 'Do you want to quit the norton commander?'.

41. Now we have completed the step of making the partition and install MSDOS operating systems. To try the MSDOS Operating Systems, Close **MyOS [Running] – Oracle VM VirtualBox** windows, you can click close button ('X') in the right-top of it.

Figure 2.57. Make Partition – 28

42. In **the Close Virtual Machine** window, tick '*power off the machine*' radio button.

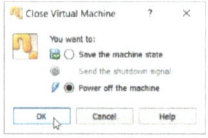

Figure 2.58. Make Partition – 29

43.   And then click the OK button.

44.   To disconnect bootable USB flashdisk from the MyOS
       Virtual machine, right-click on the top of MyOS, and then
       click **settings…**

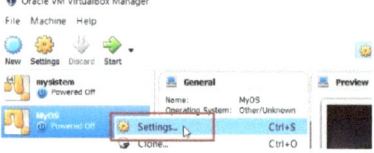

Figure 2.59. Make Partition – 30

45.   In **the MyOS – Settings** window, choose **storage** menu
       from the left. Click **usb_disk1.vmdk** in the **Storage tree**
       areas.

46.   And then click the **removes selected storage attachment**
       button to remove **usb_disk1.vmdk** controller.

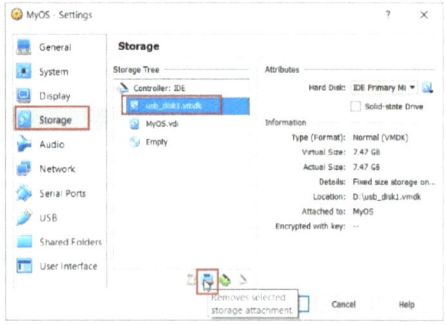

Figure 2.60. Make Partition – 31

47. Next, we change attributes of MyOS.vdi controller to *IDE Primary Master.*

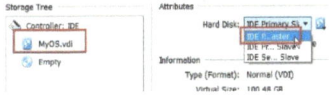

Figure 2.61. Make Partition – 32

48. And then click the OK button to save it.

49. Remove your bootable usb flashdisk from the computer or your laptop.

50. Start MyOS machine without bootable USB Flashdisk. If nothing wrong you get a display like figure 2.29. Now we already have a MSDOS operating system in MyOS virtual machines.

*****

DELETE PARTITION USING RANISH PARTITION MANAGER (PART240) APPLICATION

May be you will ask, How about a real computer ?

For real computer are not much different step. But, if you are using not empty hard disk, so you must delete all of the partition using part240 application. Here's the step to delete partition using part240 application (do not forget to backup all of your data)

1. Shutdown your computer.

2. Connect your bootable USB Flashdisk to your computer.

3. Restart your computer and get to the BIOS menu.

4. Set bootable USB flasdisk to be the first booting from your BIOS's computer and then restart your computer. Wait until

the MSDOS prompt show up like below.

Figure 2.62. Make Partition (real computer / RC) - 33

5. Type the coding below to open **Ranish Partition Manager (part240)** application.

```
cd\part240
part
```

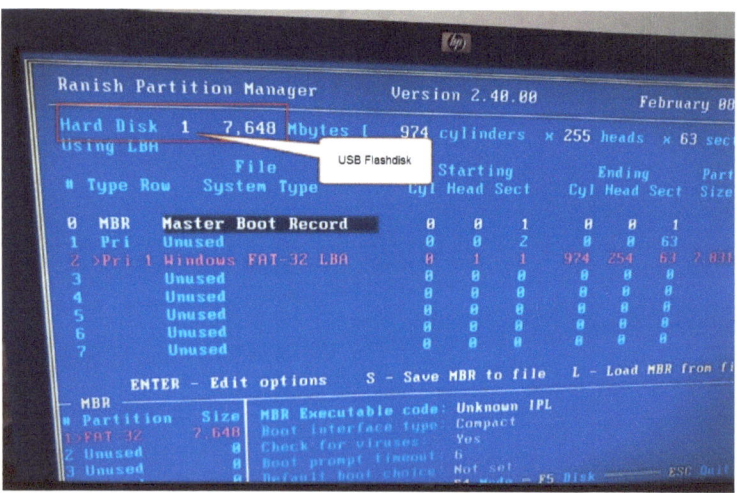

Figure 2.63. Make Partition (real computer / RC) - 34

6. In the **Ranish Partition Manager** window, press 'F5' from

your keyboard to change hard disk to the second hard disk
(hdd).

Figure 2.64. Make Partition (real computer / RC) - 35

7. Move your cursor using the up and down arrow to the
    partition.

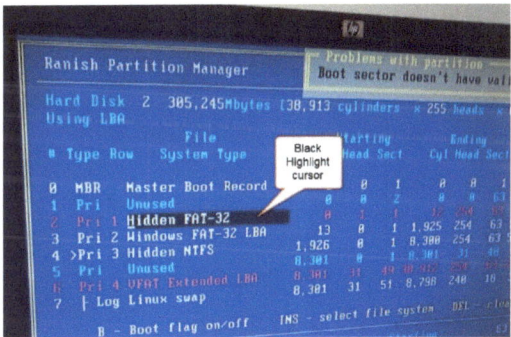

Figure 2.65. Make Partition (real computer / RC) - 36

8. Press 'Delete' key from your keyboard *to delete one-by-
    one all of the partition*, take a look at some figures below.

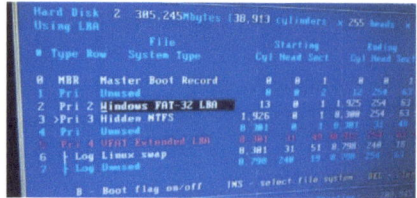

Figure 2.66. Make Partition (real computer / RC) - 37

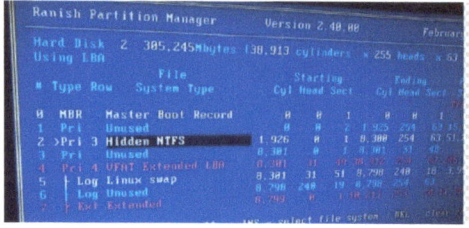

Figure 2.67. Make Partition (real computer / RC) - 38

Remove the *black* cursor and press '**delete**' key from your keyboard again and again, so it loks like the figure below.

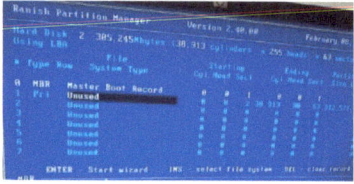

Figure 2.68. Make Partition (real computer / RC) - 39

9.   Press '**F2**' key from your keyboard to save the change.

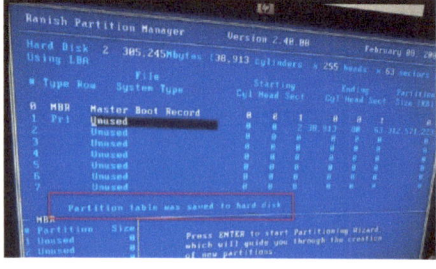

Figure 2.69. Make Partition (real computer / RC) - 40

10. Press 'ESC' key to exit from the Ranish Partition Manager.

11. Now, all of your hard disk partition has been deleted.

12. To start making a new partition, type the coding below (*that is the same step to making new partition in the virtualbox, look at to the point 4 and figure 2.30*)

```
Cd\pm80
Pqmagic
```

13. In the PowerQuest PartitionMagic 8.0 window, change disk1 (usb) to disk2 (hdd computer).

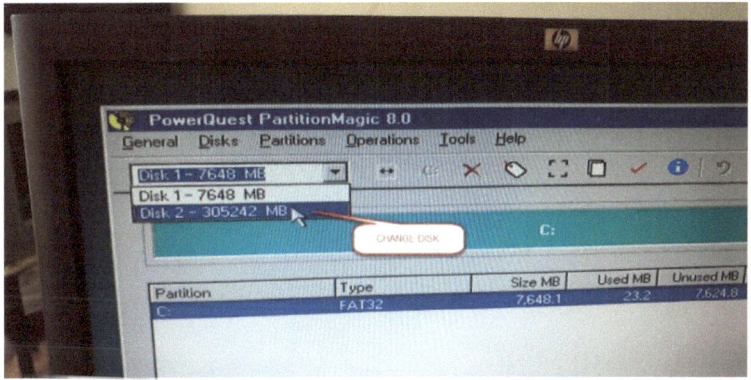

Figure 2.70. Make Partition (real computer / RC) - 41

14. And then you can follow the next step like making partition in virtualbox machines. You can define the size of each partition you want. I usually use for MSDOS 200 MB size, 50 GB for Windows 10, 30 GB for Linux Mint and the rest for data (2 primary partition and 1 extended partition)

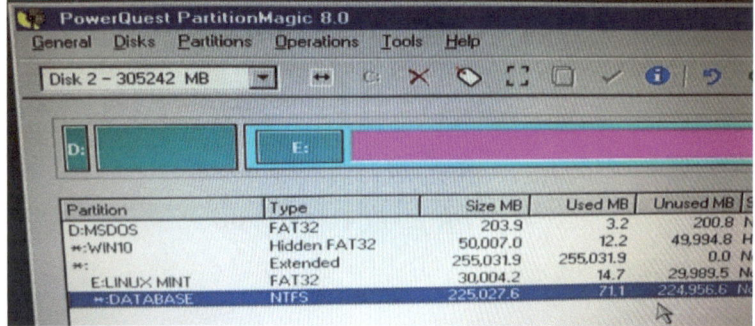

Figure 2.71. Make Partition (real computer / RC) - 42

15. After reboot your computer, you can follow steps chapter 2 sections 29-40 (above) to format and transfer MSDOS system into your hard disk computer (it is the same step).

*****

Chapter Three

INSTALLING WINDOWS

W*e had been creating some partitions, installing MSDOS Operating Systems and now in the next step is to install Windows Operating Systems.* In the real computer (PC / laptop), you need a Window Orginal Compaq Disk. But, in the VirtualBox you need ISO file of windows OS. If you have a Window Orginial Compaq Disk, convert it into ISO file. You can use MagicISO Application which can be downloaded at http://www.magiciso.com/download.htm to convert.

In this step, i use Window ISO File which can be downloaded

at http://pcriver.com/operating-systems/windows-xp-iso-download/. here's step by step to install Windows Operating Systems.

1. Reboot or restart your computer or MyOS Virtual Machine, wait until 'C:\>' prompt show up.

2. Type the coding below to open **Ranish Partition Manager** Application.

```
cd\part240
part
```

```
Microsoft(R) Windows 98
  (C)Copyright Microsoft Corp 1981-1998.

C:\>cd\part240

C:\PART240>part_
```

Figure 3.1. The Coding to Open Ranish Partition Manager

3. Now, in the Ranish Partition Manager window, move *the black cursor* into MSDOS partition (Pri 1).

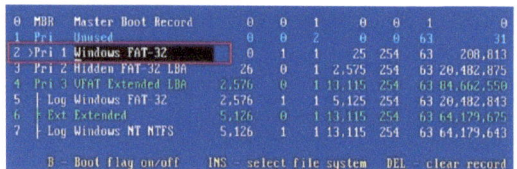

Figure 3.2. Choose MSDOS Partition (pri 1)

4. Press 'H' key from your keyboard. This action will hide MSDOS Partition.

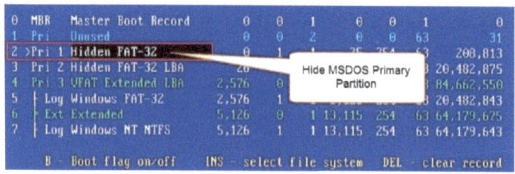

Figure 3.3. Hide MSDOS Partition (pri 1)

5.   Move to Partition 2 (pri 2). In this partition we will install the windows operating system.

6.   Press 'H' key to *Unhide* this partition. The 'H' key can be used to *hide* or *unhide* the partitions.

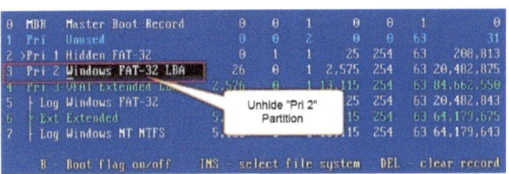

Figure 3.3. Unhide "Pri 2" Partition

7.   Because we want to install Windows Operating System in the "pri 2" partition, so press "B" key from your keyboard to make "pri 2" partition as a boot (To start the system from this partition). You can see the ">" mark in the "pri 2" partition now. The ">" mark given to a partition that is used for booting.

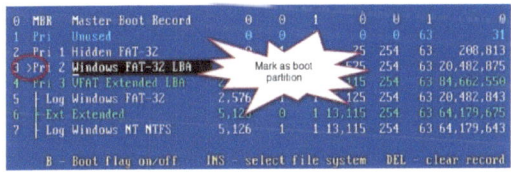

Figure 3.4. The "pri 2" Partition mark as a boot partition

8.   And then, press 'F2' key from your keyboard to save the changes.

9.   Press 'ESC' key to exit from Ranish Partition Manager.

10.   In the VirtualBox , shutdown your virtual machine.

11. In the real computer, insert Windows CD into your CD Rom. Restart your computer and follow the step install as usually or you can follow the step install window to VirtualBox machine.

12. Open setting window for MyOS Virtual machine.

13. Go to *storage* and click icon CD in **Storage Tree – Conroller: IDE**.

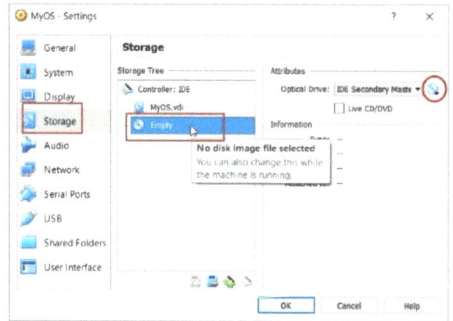

Figure 3.5. Storage CD virtual Controller

14. In **the attributes – Optical Drive**, click icon CD.

15. Choose **Virtual Optical Disk file** to open ISO file.

Figure 3.6. Choose Virtual Optical Disk File

16. In the **Please choose a virtual optical disk file** windows, choose the Window ISO file that has been downloaded previously.

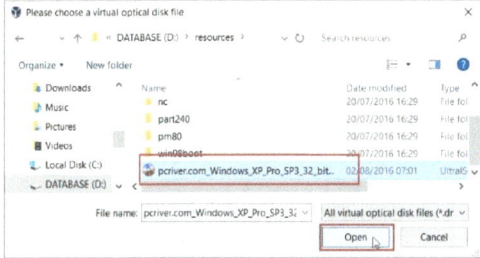

Figure 3.7. Choose the Window ISO file

17.   And then, click the **Open** button. Now, in the **Controller: IDE**, Window iso file has been on the icon CD.

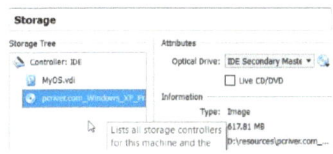

Figure 3.8. Storage Tree – Controller: IDE

18.   Click the OK button.

19.   Start the MyOS virtual machine now.

20.   In the message '*press any key to boot from CD...*', you press any key on the keyboard quickly. Wait until the figure show up below.

Figure 3.9. Windows OS Install - 01

21. Move the 'white cursor' to the Partition2.

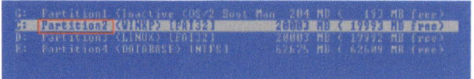

Figure 3.10. Windows OS Install - 02

22. Press 'ENTER' to install.

23. Next, choose '*convert the partition to NTFS*'.

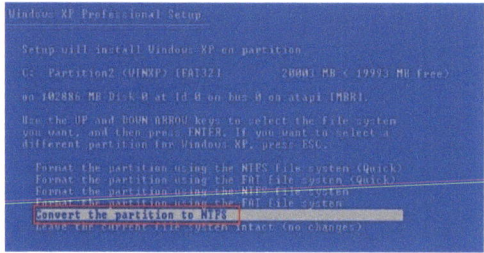

Figure 3.11. Windows OS Install - 03

24. Press 'ENTER' to continue. The install process will take place automatically, when the computer restart and display a message '*press any key to boot from CD...*' leave it alone (do not press any key) until the install continued.

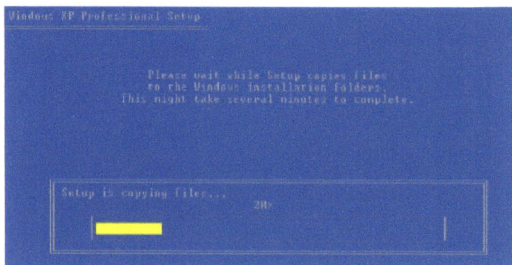

Figure 3.12. Windows OS Install - 04

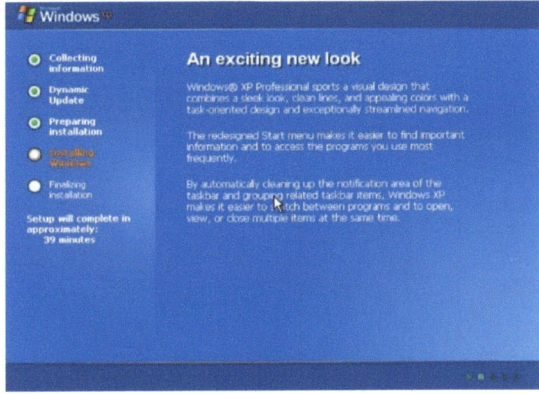

Figure 3.13. Windows OS Install - 05

25. In the **Regional and Language Options** window, click the **Next** button.

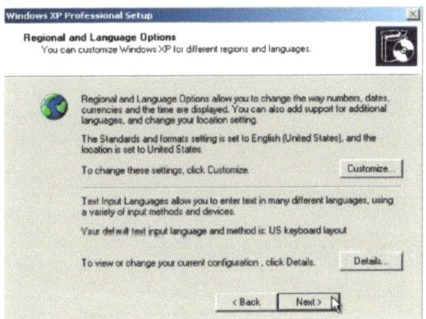

Figure 3.14. Windows OS Install - 06

26. In the **Personalize Your Software** window, input your name and organization and then click the Next button.

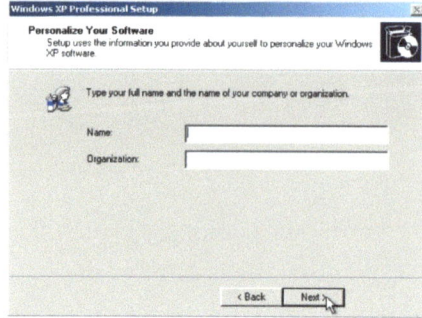

Figure 3.15. Windows OS Install - 07

27. In the **Computer Name and Administrator Password** window, you can input what do you want. Then click the Next button Again.

28. In the **Date and Time Settings** windows, you can set date, time and time zone. Click the next button.

29. In the Workgroup or computer domain window, you can enter your workgroup name. And then click the next button again.

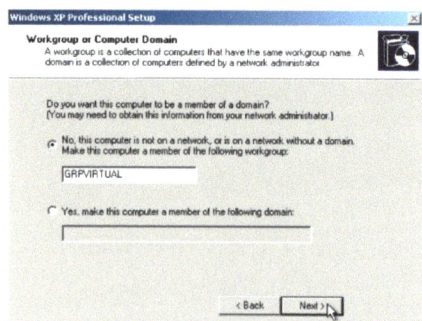

Figure 3.16. Windows OS Install - 08

30. You can follow the steps install like usually, until you can see the main windows Xp like below.

Figure 3.17. Windows OS Install - 09

31. Now, if you restart the MyOS virtual machine without pressing any buttons, you will be automatically entered into Windows XP Operating System.

*****

Chapter Four

INSTALLING LINUX MINT

To install Linux Mint, we have to go back into the MSDOS Operating systems. Here's step by step to go back into MSDOS Operating systems and install Linux Mint.

1. In the Real Computer, use your BIOS setting to set boot from USB flashdisk.

2. In the VirtualBox.

    a. Open MyOS – Settings.

    b. In the *Storage – Controller: IDE*, remove virtual disk file that we use to install Window XP.

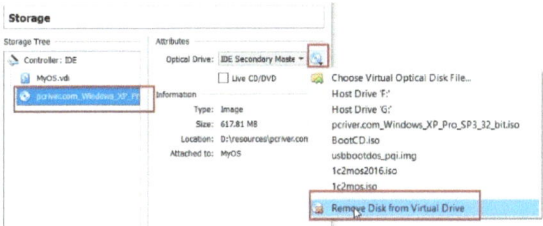

Figure 4.1. Remove Disk from Virtual Drive

c. After remove, the icon of Compaq Disk show 'empty' label. Add a **usb_disk1.vmdk** virtual file as described previously in chapter 2 section 3.2 (f-n) above until figure 2.27.

d. Click the start button from the top menu to start MyOS virtual machine (figure 2.28).

e. In the 'C:\>' prompt, type the coding to open **Ranish Partition Manager**.

```
Microsoft(R) Windows 98
    (C)Copyright Microsoft Corp 1981-1998.

C:\>cd\part240

C:\PART240>part_
```

Figure 4.2. The coding to open Ranish Partition Manager

f. In **the Ranish Partition Manager** Window (see figure 2.63), press '**F5**' key from your keyboard to activate **Disk 2** (HDD virtual disk)

g. Move the 'black cursor' into MSDOS Partition (pri 1).

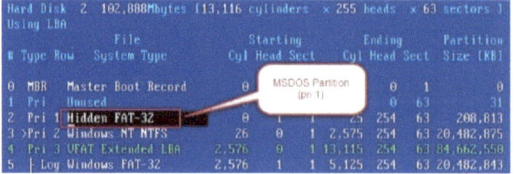

Figure 4.3. MSDOS Partition (pri 1)

h. Press 'H' key to **unhide** the partition.

i. Press 'B' key to make the partition as a boot.

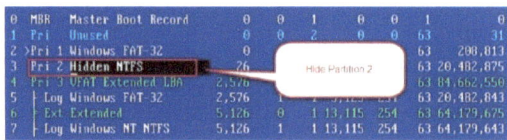

Figure 4.4. Making MSDOS Partition (pri 1) unhide and boot

j. Move the 'black cursor' to Partition 2 (pri 2).

k. Press 'H' to *hide* the partition 2.

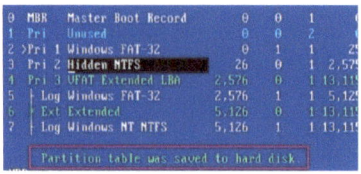

Figure 4.5. Making Partition 2 (pri 2) hide

l. Press 'F2' key from keyboard to save the changes.

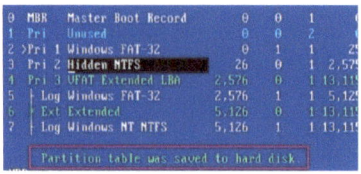

Figure 4.6. Label of Saved Partition

58

m. Press 'ESC' to exit from Ranish Partition Manager.

n. Shutdown or close MyOS Virtual Machines.

o. To disconnect bootable USB Flashdisk from the Virtual Machine, you can follow chapter 2 steps 44 – 50.

3. Shutdown and close the virtual machine again. We want to add Linux Mint ISO file into MyOS virtual machine.

4. Download Linux Mint ISO File from the link below.

https://www.linuxmint.com/download.php

5. To add Linux Mint ISO File into MyOS Virtual Machine, you can follow in chapter 3 steps 12 – 18. But, in the step 16, you choose The Linux Mint ISO File like figure below.

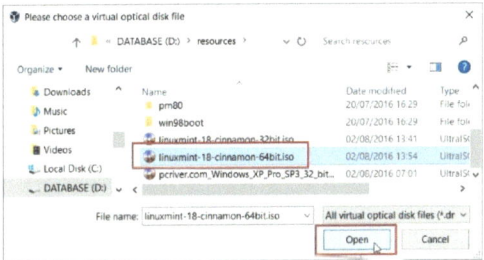

Figure 4.7. Add the Linux Mint ISO File

6. And then, start MyOS virtual machine now.

7. In the beginning logo of Linux Mint, Press any key Quicly to enter the menu.

Figure 4.8. The Beginning logo of Linux Mint

8. In the **Welcome to Linux Mint 18 Cinamon 64-bit** window, choose ***Start Linux Mint*** and then press 'ENTER' key from your keyboard.

Figure 4.9. Welcome to Linux Mint 18 Cinamon

9. In the **Linux Mint main window**, you can double click to the icon **Install Linux Mint**.

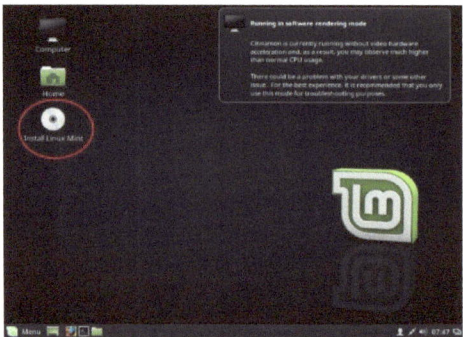

Figure 4.10. Linux Mint 18 Cinamon Main Window

10. In the **Welcome** window, click the **continue** button.

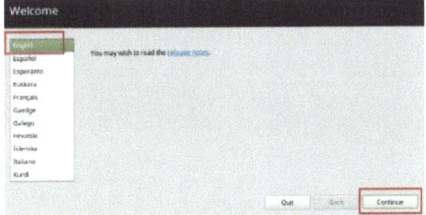

Figure 4.11. Installing Linux Mint - 01

11. In the **Preparing to install Linux Mint** window, click the **continue** button again.

12. In the **Installation type** window, choose '*Something else*' radio button.

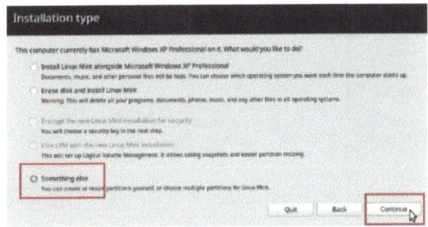

Figure 4.12. Installing Linux Mint - 02

13. Click the **continue** button.

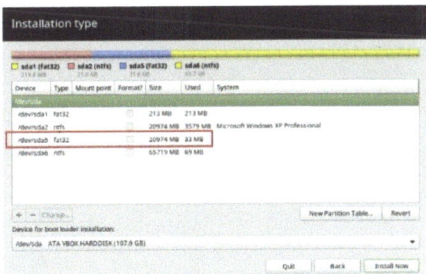

Figure 4.13. Installing Linux Mint - 03

14. You can see in the figure 4.13, we will install linux mint into device: **/dev/sda5** and type: **fat 32**. Click that device.

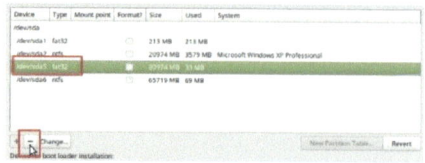

Figure 4.14. Installing Linux Mint - 04

15. And then click the '-' button (look at the left bottom of figure 4.14) to **delete** this partition.

Figure 4.15. Installing Linux Mint - 05

16. Click the *free space* device (figure 4.15).

17. And then click the '+' button (look at the left bottom of figure 4.15) to create some partitions for linux mint.

18. In the **Create Partition** window, type 4096 MB for the swap area. (RAM 2048 x 2 = 4096 MB). You can follow the data entered below.

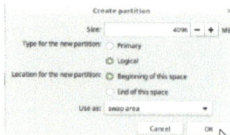

Figure 4.16. Installing Linux Mint - 06

Size: **4096**

Type for the new partition: **Logical**

Location for the new partition: **Beginning of this space**

Use as: **Swap area**

19.   Click the **OK** button to save the change. The Result can be seen below.

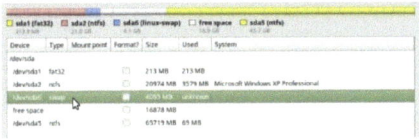

Figure 4.17. Installing Linux Mint - 07

20.   Click the *free space* device again.

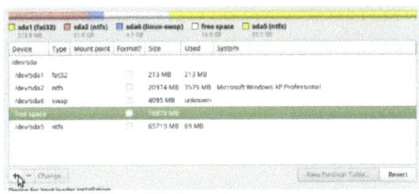

Figure 4.18. Installing Linux Mint - 08

21.   Click the '+' button again to make the next partition. You can set The second partition of linux mint like below.

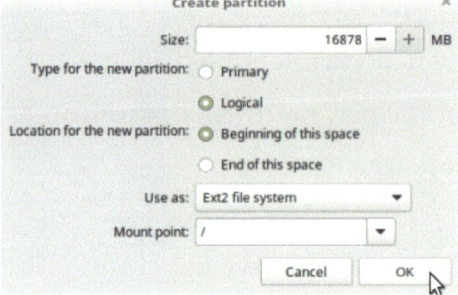

Figure 4.19. Installing Linux Mint - 09

Size: (**do not change / use of all size**)

Type for the new partition: **Logical**

Location for the new partition: **Beginning of this space**

Use as: **Ext2 file system**

Mount point: /

22.   Click the **OK** button to save.

Figure 4.20. Installing Linux Mint - 10

23.   Now, set the **Device for boot loader installation:** to /**dev/sda7**

With this setting, the linux mint can only run when we call the system partition. (we will call the system from MasterBooter Application).

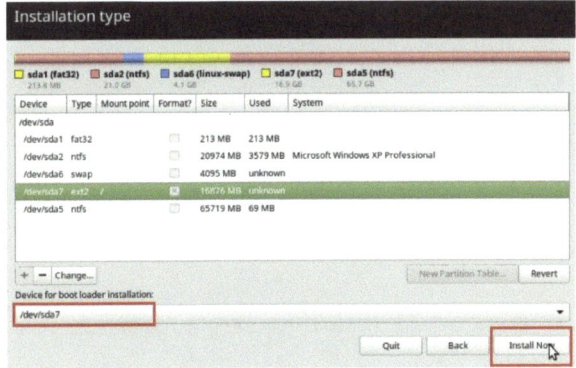

Figure 4.21. Installing Linux Mint - 11

24. Click the **Install Now** button to start installation of Linux Mint.

25. In the **Write the changes to disks?** Window, click the **continue** button.

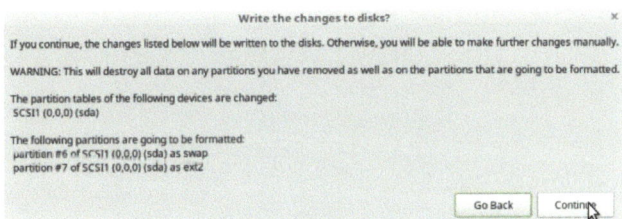

Figure 4.22. Installing Linux Mint - 12

26. In the **where are you?** Window, click your country area.

27. Click the **Continue** button.

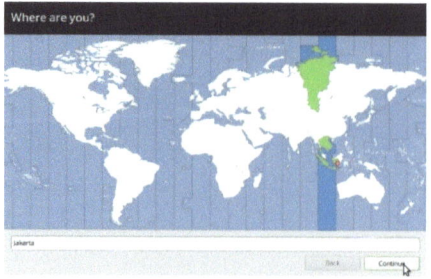

Figure 4.23. Installing Linux Mint - 13

28.   In the **Keyboard layout** window, choose your keyboard layout, and then click the **Continue** button.

29.   In the **Who are you?** Window, you can input **your name, computer's name, username, choose a password** and **confirm your password**.

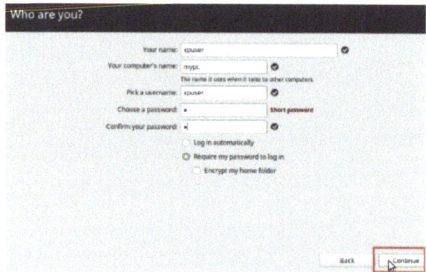

Figure 4.24. Installing Linux Mint - 14

30.   Next, click the **Continue** button again. And then we wait until the install is completed.

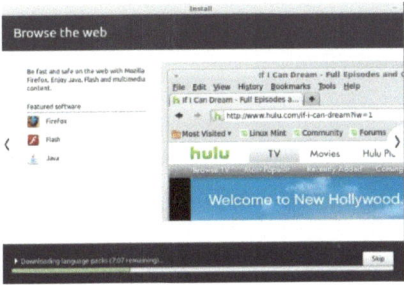

Figure 4.25. Installing Linux Mint - 15

31.   In the **Installation Complete** window, click the **Restart Now** button.

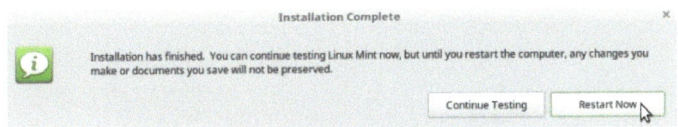

Figure 4.26. Installing Linux Mint - 16

32.   If you see the message '*please remove the installation medium, then press ENTER:*', close the MyOS Virtual Machine.

Figure 4.27. Installing Linux Mint - 17

33.   You can follow the steps 2 section a – d (see figure 4.1) to remove virtual compaq disk files (ISO file) from the virtual

machine. But, if it is empty, you can to skip this steps.

34.   After restart, you will only see MSDOS Operating system like figure 2.29 ('C:\>' prompt). We can to use MasterBooter application to open Linux Mint.

*****

Chapter Five

INSTALLING MASTERBOOTER

T*he operating systems often have their own unique loader code, and won't let you use other systems, unless you know tricky methods to get past this.* MasterBooter works by replacing the program in the MBR with its own loader code that you can configure, so you can select from any installed operating systems (Daniel, Nagy: masterbooter.com).

With MasterBooter we can choose, secure and use the operating system as desired. Here's step by step to install

MasterBooter.

1.   In the 'C:\>' prompt, type the coding below to open MasterBooter.

```
cd\mrboot
mrbooter
```

```
Microsoft(R) Windows 98
    (C)Copyright Microsoft Corp 1981-1998.

C:\>cd\mrboot

C:\MRBOOT>mrbooter_
```

Figure 5.1. Installing MasterBooter - 01

2.   In the **MasterBooter** window, you can see all of primary partition and logical partition that has the operating systems.

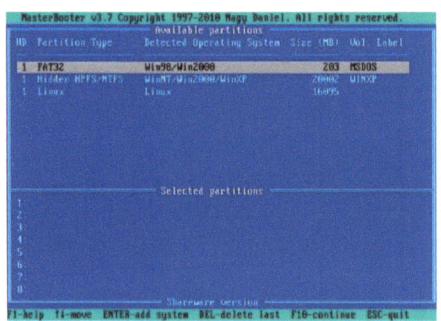

Figure 5.2. Installing MasterBooter - 02

3.   Press the '**ENTER**' key from your keyboard to choose or selected primary partition that has the operating systems in the **available partitions** box. You can select one by one untill all of the operating systems are enter in the **selected**

partition box.

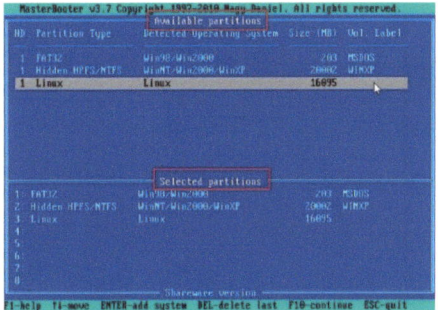

Figure 5.3. Installing MasterBooter - 03

4.   Press 'F10' key from your keyboard to continue.

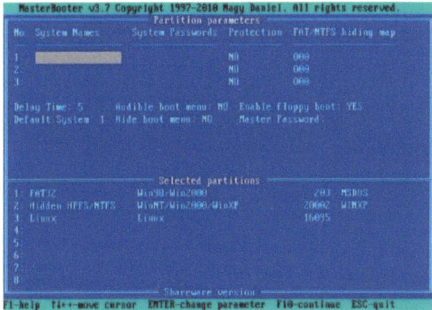

Figure 5.4. Installing MasterBooter - 04

In figure 5.4, we can see there are 2 main box is a system parameter and the selected partition. Number 1 on the system parameter represents the number 1 in the selected partition as well as number 2 and 3.

5.   **Number 1** will have the name MSDOS V98. Press 'ENTER' to type that name in the **system names** box.

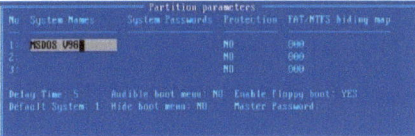

Figure 5.5. Installing MasterBooter - 05

6.   After type the name, press 'ENTER' to save.

7.   And the move the 'white' cursor to the **system passwords**.
      To move the cursor, you use up, down, left and right arrows
      on your keyboard. Press 'ENTER' to type your password
      here, however, if you intend not to give the password then
      skip this input box.

8.   Move your cursor again to the **Protection** section. In this
      section, you are asked to enter the keyboard keys
      combination to secure the system. If you activate this
      protection, the systems will be hidden and will not be
      shown in the start menu until the user presses the keyboard
      keys combination that have been created. To disable this
      secure function, you can press 'ENTER' key from your
      keyboard.

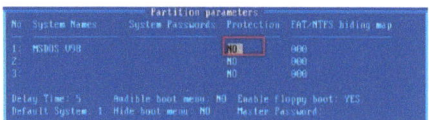

Figure 5.6. Installing MasterBooter - 06

9.   Move your cursor to the **FAT/NTFS hiding map**. In this
      section, we can choose which partition to be displayed
      (*unhide=0* or *hide=1*) in conjunction with a system that is
      activated or selected by the user. Each digit in the input box
      representing sequence on the selected partition box. The
      first number 0 representing the first partition on the
      selected partition box. The second 0 representing the

second partition on the selected partition box, as well as the third 0.

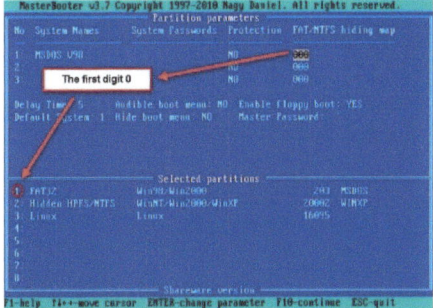

Figure 5.7. Installing MasterBooter – 07

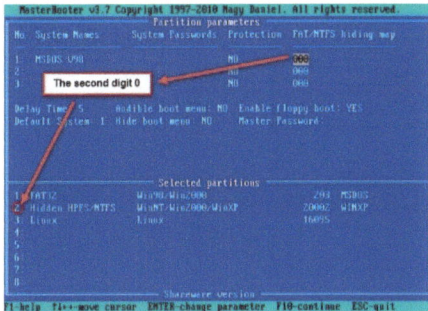

Figure 5.8. Installing MasterBooter – 08

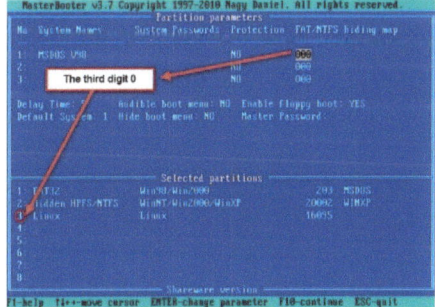

Figure 5.9. Installing MasterBooter – 09

10. Now, if we want when MSDOS Operating system is running, then the partition windows and linux become hide.

Then setting digit should we make is 011. Press 'ENTER' key to type 011 in the **FAT/NTFS hiding map** input box. Press 'Enter' again to save it.

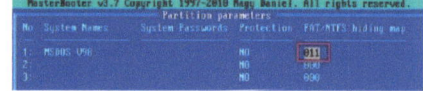

Figure 5.10. Installing MasterBooter – 10

11. In the **number 2** partition parameters, we give sytem name is WINDOWS XP.

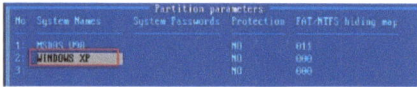

Figure 5.11. Installing MasterBooter – 11

12. In the **System Passwords** input box, we type 12345 as the password keys.

13. For now, we do not give a protection, so skip this column.

14. In the **FAT/NTFS hiding map** input box, we type 100. The first digit 1 that mean is we hide MSDOS Partition (partition 1). The second digit 0 that mean is unhide for windows xp partition (partition 2) and the thirds mean is unhide for linux mint partition. Linux Mint partition has two logical partition. If we unhide this partition, it is mean both logical partition will be activated. However, Windows can only read the second partition (DATABASE / ntfs) whereas linux partition will not be readable by windows.

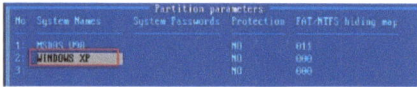

Figure 5.12. Installing MasterBooter – 12

15. In the **Number 3** Partition parameters. We give system name is **Linux Mint**.

16. In the **System Passwords**, we give 1 as the password key.

17. We skip the Protection column.

18. In the **FAT/NTFS hiding map**, we type 110. That is mean, we hide MSDOS and Windows partition.

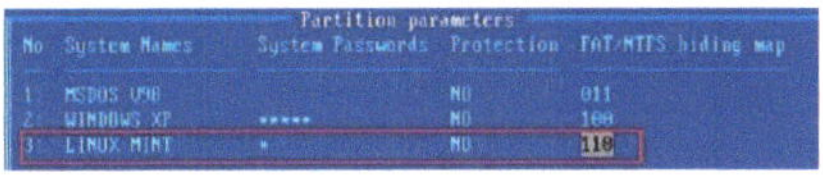

Figure 5.13. Installing MasterBooter – 13

19. Move the 'white' cursor to the **Delay Time** input box.

20. Press 'ENTER' key.

21. Type 20 to delay time. User only have 20 seconds to choose one system. If time runs out and the user has not chosen any of the existing system then automatically **Default System** wil run. Press 'ENTER' key again to save.

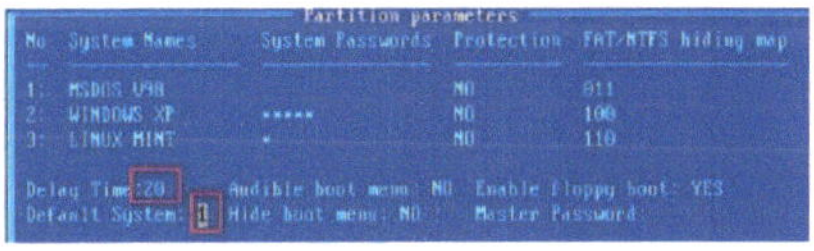

Figure 5.14. Installing MasterBooter – 14

In the figure 5.14, Default system is 1. It means, MSDOS operating system as the default system.

22. Do not make changes to the Audible Boot Menu and Enable Floppy boot unless you want it.

23. In the **hide boot menu** input box, we can set YES to make hiding list of system menu. But this is **only available in the registered version only**.

24. The Master Password is used to provide security at the application MasterBooter. Each time the application is opened automatically you will be prompted to enter a password.

25. Press 'F10' to Continue.

26. In the message '*Are you sure to save these setting?...*', press 'Y' to save the changes.

27. Press any key to reboot. After reboot, we will see list of system menu like below.

![MasterBooter v3.7 — Choose a system: 1: MSDOS V98, 2: WINDOWS XP, 3: LINUX MINT. Time left: 15. SHAREWARE! Please register!]

Figure 5.15. MasterBooter List of System Menu

*If we can set the **Hide Boot Menu** (steps 23) to 'Yes' then the computer will not display the menu, just a blank screen and when the time runs out will automatically running the **Default System**. The menu will be displayed if you press the **key combination** that is stored at the facility hide boot menu. So the other users will say '...ooh this computer only has MSDOS operating system....'.*

28. Choose and click MSDOS V98 from the list menu. Because this operating system does not have a password then automatically we can get into the MSDOS operating system.

29. Restart you computer again.

30. And then choose and click Windows XP from the list menu.

Figure 5.16. Windows XP label menu

31. Because we have set a password then we can see password box like figure below. Type your password here (at step 12, the password is 12345).

Figure 5.17. Enter Password box

*Each character you has typed into this box **can not be delete (undone)**, so if you has typed a wrong character just press 'ENTER' key to repeat all entry input character. The system just to show 'Bad. Try Again...' label.*

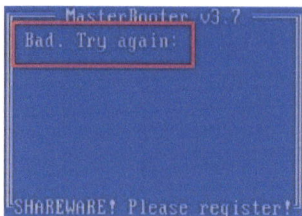

Figure 5.18. Label of wrong password

32. If we enter the wrong password three times, it will are presented in the message '*sorry, access denied!*'. Just restart your computer to go to MasterBooter list of system menu again.

33. If we enter the correct password, then we will be able to open Windows XP operating system. Now, you can check in the Windows Explorer application to see Database Partition (logical partition). But we can not see the Linux Mint Partition.

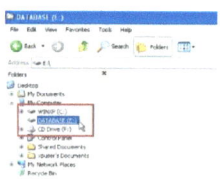

Figure 5.19. Database Partition on Windows XP

34. Database Partition can also be seen in Linux Mint Operating System. If you set the **FAT/NTFS hiding map** to '000' (step 18) then you can see also MSDOS and Windows Partition. It is depend to your setting.

Chapter Six

UNINSTALLING MASTERBOOTER

You can create your own settings about how *the behaviour of MasterBooter in order to fulfill your will.* But, if you want to uninstall this application, you can follow the step below.

1. Enter to the MSDOS Operating System.
2. Type the coding below to open MasterBooter Application.

```
cd\mrboot
efdisk /mbr
```

```
Microsoft(R) Windows 98
    (C)Copyright Microsoft Corp 1981-1998.

C:\>cd\mrboot

C:\MRBOOT>efdisk /mbr_
```

Figure 6.1. Uninstalling Masterbooter - 01

3. If you press the 'ENTER' key, it will automatically be cleared the MasterBooter Application from Master Boot Record (MBR) and the Default System is taking the action.

```
Microsoft(R) Windows 98
    (C)Copyright Microsoft Corp 1981-1998.

C:\>cd\mrboot

C:\MRBOOT>efdisk /mbr
New MBR loader has been installed successfully.
C:\MRBOOT>_
```

Figure 6.2. Uninstalling Masterbooter - 02

4. If you restart your computer then you will be in MSDOS Operating Systems.

*****

About the Author

Aryanto. Born in Sungai Menang August 14, 1974. He studied Accounting Department at Economics Faculty of SRIWIJAYA UNIVERSITY (Bachelor Degree/S1 - 1999) and Master of Information Technology Department at Computer Faculty of INDONESIA UNIVERITY (2010). Until now there were more than four works have in him, among others: (1) Database

Programming with Microsoft Visual FoxPro, (2) Network Programming with Microsoft Visual FoxPro, (3) Tips and Tricks Programming Professional with Microsoft Visual FoxPro, and (4) BS MySQL Database Programming with Microsoft Visual FoxPro. Contribute in the field of programming by making the MIS hospitals in 1999 and the hospital payroll program (1999). He is currently working at the Economics Faculty of Sriwijaya University.

He has made several ebook like below (you can find with the 'aryanto' key on play book google).

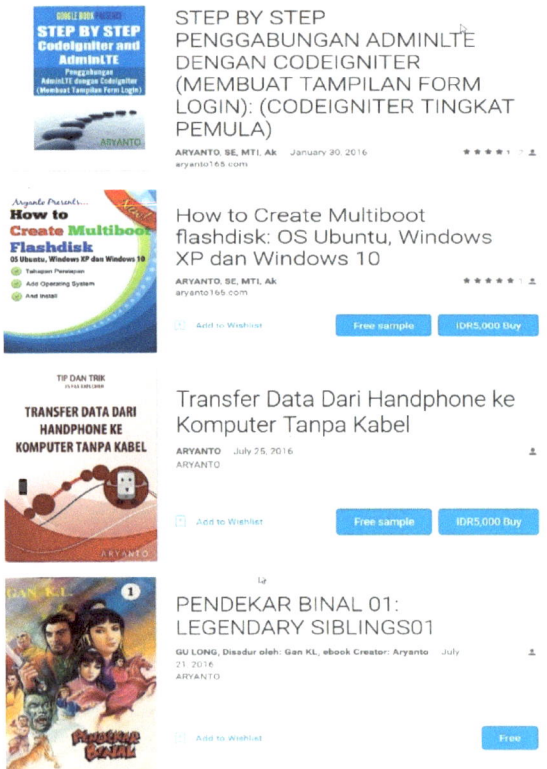

STEP BY STEP PENGGABUNGAN ADMINLTE DENGAN CODEIGNITER (MEMBUAT TAMPILAN FORM LOGIN): (CODEIGNITER TINGKAT PEMULA)

ARYANTO, SE, MTI, Ak   January 30, 2016
aryanto165.com

How to Create Multiboot flashdisk: OS Ubuntu, Windows XP dan Windows 10

ARYANTO, SE, MTI, Ak
aryanto165.com

Add to Wishlist   Free sample   IDR5,000 Buy

Transfer Data Dari Handphone ke Komputer Tanpa Kabel

ARYANTO   July 25, 2016
ARYANTO

Add to Wishlist   Free sample   IDR5,000 Buy

PENDEKAR BINAL 01: LEGENDARY SIBLINGS01

GU LONG, Disadur oleh: Gan KL, ebook Creator: Aryanto   July 21, 2016
ARYANTO

Add to Wishlist   Free

A R Y A N T O

Soal Latihan dan Jawaban
Pengolahan Database MySQL
Tingkat Dasar

Aryanto February 1, 2016

Dnnnublich

Add to Wishlist

In the Amazon.com

How to Create multiboot Flashdisk: OS Ubuntu, Windows XP and Windows 10
(Indonesian Edition) Mar 4, 2016
by Aryanto Ardo

Paperback
$7.00 *Prime*
Get it by **Thursday, Aug 4**

FREE Shipping on eligible orders
Books: See all 4 items

www.aryanto165.com

Thanks for reading! Please add a short review on Amazon, Kindle, itunes, play book google and let me know what you thought!

You can see the results that you will earn or learn from this book at the link below.
Hide masterbooter list menu
https://www.youtube.com/watch?v=Z86ev03FMl8

hide one of the operating system from masterbooter list menu
https://www.youtube.com/watch?v=EgspFADzccg

How to setup master booter
https://www.youtube.com/watch?v=IyYEN44N3cI

If you have difficulties in understanding the content of this book, please do not hesitate to send an email to:
ARNILA@YAHOO.COM
or
ARNILA2008@GMAIL.COM.

Thanks and good luck!
Aryanto

www.ingramcontent.com/pod-product-compliance
Lightning Source LLC
Chambersburg PA
CBHW040829180526
45159CB00001B/116